more

Shoot the Alligators

MW00911587

Some poets are born of the fire that makes the world in all of its beautiful doom, Stolte is one of those poets - let him sing.
—RA Washington, author of *BLACK Eunuch*

Nathanael Stolte's new collection, *Shoot the Alligators Closest to the Boat*, is right up my alley. It has guts. It's accessible. There's more here than just that, however. There is also craft, beautiful imagery, and poems that stick with you long after reading them. It's a hell of a collection, and I can't recommend it highly enough.
—Daniel Crocker, author of *Leadwood*

'Nathanael William Stolte always has room for you in his heart. It's warm and metaphysical in there, so be sure to bring your slippers and a flask. Stolte is the everyday-man's man, writing of a simple and humble life. He is often brave enough to call people out on their shit (including his own), writing, "Being wrong is a universal human condition." His short pieces land like grenades and his longer pieces spin tales of the intricacies of aging, the nature of perspective, and lessons necessary for becoming a better person. Wherever Stolte may be, I am confident that he is experiencing and writing about that place in its most beautifully authentic form. Like the city, this collection is dirty and tough, mysterious and sentimental. Stolte characterizes his collection well when he writes, "It's cold / my feet are wet & / I wouldn't change a thing."
—Linzi Garcia, author of *Thank You*

Stolte shows us his favorite parts of hell with calm enthusiasm. His love affair with perdition cools with distance from the inferno, but still proves eternal. There is humor and humility in this complex (but not convoluted) collection of street-kid war stories and dope sick love letters. It reads like a lullaby for the damned.
—Ezhno Martín, founding editor EMP Books

In my favorite poem in this collection, Stolte laments "I have never loved deeply enough to truly break / I hope someday I can be strong like Barb / & shatter". I hesitate to call anyone a liar, especially a poet, but I have my doubts. Reading this extraordinary collection, it seems clear to me that the poet is already like Barb. Describing your own shortcomings brutally takes strength. Looking gray brothers and night children in the eye is a kind of love, and a deep one at that. And as for breaking, I think the poet already has~but only in that breaking and breaking open are often the same thing. Poetry and prayer go together, like honey and coffee. This book is a prayer book, in the best kind of way. I feel this in my gut, but that does lead to the question, what is this a prayer for? It is a prayer for trying, sometimes succeeding, but always in trying there is redemption. Read this book.
—Nadia Wolnisty, EIC of Thimble Lit Mag

Shoot the Alligators Closest to the Boat

poems by

Nathanael William Stolte

STUBBORN MULE PRESS
DEVIL'S ELBOW, MO

Stubborn Mule Press

Devil's Elbow, MO

stubbornmulepress.com

Copyright (c) 2019 Nathanael William Stolte

First Edition 11 7 5 3 2 1

ISBN: 978-1-950380-13-8

LCCN: 2019935876

Design, edits and layout: Jason Ryberg, Jeanette Powers

stubbornmulepress@gmail.com

@stubbornmulepress

Cover Image: Elim J. Sidus

Interior Photo Credit: Nathanael Stolte

Author photo: painting by Jeanette Powers: *Nathanael Watches Over the Pigeons*

For Maj Ragain (September 15, 1940- April 19, 2018)
Down the road

Contents

My old friend morphine
keeps all kinds of pain at bay
but brings his own pain

FRIDAY THE 13TH, OCTOBER 2006

That was the autumn the rains
came off the Lake without apology
while trees were yet burdened with leaf

When shelter & comfort of
the burning stream of corn whisky
solace in solidarity & filth

As thundersnow draped
three & a half feet of wet blanket on
the City of Good Neighbors

When the sun quit
me & the city blacked out
but the squats never lost power

The Sabers still
played the Rangers
we go hard in the Nickel City

Tops Market had their lights cut by
overburdened power-lines & filled a
long contractor's dumpster with frozen food

We waded in
swam through it
filled the van with—

TGIFridays mozzarella sticks & onion rings
Tony's pizza & enough chicken fingers to feed
the whole subvert army for the already winter

Some people suffered
some died
but it was the trees I felt for

In a formula of
wet snow & surface area
the weight proved too much

It was the oaks that
suffered most   tall & proud
shallow roots & rigid countenance

The willows with their long fingers
deep in the earth & malleable wooden bodies
were utterly unbroken

I see them everyday
with their oak bodies
& scorn

We the subverts
are as willows—
rooted & unfazed

GIFTS UNGIVEN

When I was 15, Zack de la Rocha told me with a whisper
your anger is a gift
I didn't understand what he was giving me
I didn't understand what this meant
but I liked the way it sounded
still do
his words have stayed with me through the decades

When I was 25, Vic Ruggiero told me
every day the human race is
filling me with more disgrace
this I understood
these words have been a mantra
as I've trudged in heavy boots
through a cringe-worthy world

When I was 35, she asked me
why don't you write love poems
or poems about nature?

Darling,
every poem I write is a love poem
while Mother slowly dies
everything I do is an expression of love

Look around—
this place
the way we treat one another
the way we value
imaginary assets &
fiscal idolatry

over bodies
over trees

is a maddening disgrace
that shames us all

The modern day Atlantis is in the
Pacific Ocean
it's made of North American rubbish
it's not getting any smaller

Toxic algae blooms
choke the coastal beaches

It is said that by 2050
there will be more
plastics in the oceans
than fish

When Her last hummingbird
fills the air with its final poetry
will we regret what we've swapped?

When the last great whale
washes ashore
with a belly full of plastic
will it curse us with its final breath?

So yeah,
this is a love poem
& I am angry
& it's a gift

I LEARNED ABOUT THE BIRDS & THE BEES
FROM PORNOGRAPHY

My father never gave me the talk

I learned about sex from pornography
this was before the advent of the internet
when we had to swap magazines we stole from
the very fathers that—
were too embarrassed
or busy
or scared
or whatever
to teach a generation of boys
the right way to fuck a lady

Maybe their fathers are to blame

When I discovered
his skin magazines
while exploring the closets &
spider dwellings
in my childhood home
I happened upon
glossy
bright
lurid
photos
of women
in magazines
doing things
foreign to me
yet intrinsically

I knew
it was
something
special

I took the magazines
one at a time
back to my room
I never replaced
what I took
yet I took another
every day or so
Until one day
I came home from school
to find my room
turned over

All the magazines were gone

He never said a word to me about that either

There were other magazines
all text with small photos &
single panel comics that I didn't understand
but somehow knew
I shouldn't talk about them in church

Like Columbus
I discovered
something ancient

Yet new
to me

JAKE

Spent his days
collecting cans
for another bottle

When the
doctors
checked
his oil
his liver was
a couple decades
overdue

You could smell
it when he spoke

Jake
spent his nights
out front of the
can return

where they found him
one morning

rust & smoke

SAMMY

Fed the whole squat
with food stamp cards
he collected from
all over the country

Sammy added
Philly guts
to his Midnight
Special loose tobacco

a true gleaner

he understood
the value
in chaff

The gen-u-ine article

Rust Punk

His dogs always ate
before he did

He only wore
workman coveralls
he fished out of
some dumpster

Sammy always
knew which dumpsters
were biting

Knew where the
bakery filled large trash-bags
with unsold bagels at day's end

Knew where the
grocer threw away
browning produce &
expired meat

Eventually
Sammy was found
with blue lips
somewhere out west
next to a dumpster

See—
Sammy had a devil
at the switchboard

a devil in his arm

THEY TORE DOWN DEPEW SKATING & IF THEY
BUILD ANOTHER STARBUCKS OUT OF MY
GENTRIFYING CHILDHOOD
I'LL CURSE THEM

We revolved around it
in our perfect little
God-bodies
The center of
our small universe

Forming peculiar
constellations
in some angsty
alien zodiac

Now it's a
nostalgic snuff film
of cannibalized innocence
Fenced-off &
opened-up

Gutted
in some sort of
archeological autopsy
of perverse progress

As the long
dull-yellow
arms of
the excavators
dig into
my childhood's

sepulture
memories are freed
from leyline
bondage

& now
I'm being
haunted

The last
real gathering of
antiquated
constellations
was at
Snuffy's funeral
I want to remember
him like
Hale Bop Comet
a heavenly thing
that comes
only once
in a lifetime

I want to remember
him with bubble-gum-mohawk
dog-collar &
painted middle finger

I want to remember him
like a Roman-fucking-candle
throat on fire with a nihilist sound

Not the tortured maverick
they planted
with a beer belly

& no
healthcare

I want his ghost
to be young
like the remastered
version of
Return of the Jedi
where Anakin's
simulacrum
is converted
to a youth
That's the way
memory should be

Retroactively shaped
by a future that
couldn't exist
in each moment
of infinite possibility

I only want
the devil-may-care attitude

Not some husk
not some steamship
run aground &
left to hulk in atrophy

Like Depew Skating
on Transit Rd.
where we
converged every
Friday night
in coven &

community
of idolaters
& cutters

Our hair colored
with Manic Panic
& Bingo Dabbers

A holy place

Temple of Marlboros
& flannel
& ripped jeans

Where the DJ mixed
a mosaic or
90's
rap
black metal
& the
Hokey Pokey

No one ever skated
but we all glided
across the tumult
of youth with
regal clumsiness

I remember when
Kurt Cobain
Hemingway-ed
himself
we all held vigil
in an alchemy of

mascara & hot tears
because
heroin was
still myth
& the devil
hadn't yet
kissed us
on the mouth

Snuffy always
thought he
could out-dance
the devil forever

We get old
my friend &
our dance isn't
so sweet

May we all find
what we have lost   here
in this open earth

& NUCLEAR WINTER WON'T BE SO BAD AS LONG AS MICHAEL BUBLÉ HAS EXCLUSIVE RIGHTS TO THE SOUNDTRACK

—*For Troy Cloutier (Thanks for the pollen, here's some honey)*

It's winter again & Michael Bublé
has a two-for-one special on Christmas carol lobotomies
I'm working this party with my friend Troy
We are slinging *bolognaise* to the affluent &
I know they won't tip well because
they've never known the comforts of service
but I smile my bad teeth smile anyway
even though these wine-soaked bastards are really running us
Their teeth are straight & white
too white, like fresh suburban snow dreams or
New Year's resolutions that are too new to be unrealistic
Because we all know real change is small & can't be scheduled

Anyway, Bernie Sanders' identical twin is here
cleaning up a giant Jenga set into reusable shopping bags
He looks mythic in his expensive suit
kneeling down cleaning up someone else's mess
but it's really his mess too. It's everybody's mess
It's like a metaphor for America that's too obscure
for me to articulate &
wouldn't make a bit of difference anyhow
No one thinks in metaphor anymore anyway
It's all dick jokes & social stratification

But the wine keeps flowing & the scornful looks are
dimly lost in the mood lighting of the fancy shack
where we are waiting on these hogs
Then *I'm Dreaming of a White Christmas* comes on

the dining room's ubiquitous radio &
I'm running around dreaming of a day
when these white people aren't so fucking smug
At this point I almost welcome the apocalypse
because it all seems so far gone &
appealing to the humanity of the oppressors
will never bring about any change, no matter how small
These inclement weather patterns of the heart
seem more tormenting than a nuclear winter wonderland
could at this moment of feigned humility
This Bacchus of inhuman-trash-monsters &
climate change deniers was never fun to begin with &
the novelty has worn thinner than my patience for these
perfect teeth winos with their Chanel handbags &
mousy husbands who won't tip me well anyway
Sometimes I want to tell them off
tell them they are the reason the
polar ice caps are thinning out &
the ozone layer has abandoned
us humans to our own scrimshaw fates
Then I remember I'm also to blame
but I need to make rent & keep my old Buicks' belly full
so I can get where I need to be to do what needs doin'
For this I'm the same as everyone else
I'd just like someone to blame
so I can feel superior to
these mantis-people who keep running
me ragged for pennies
even if it's only for a moment

At least Troy mostly feels the same &
we can mock these tools behind their backs
when they leave & we're cleaning up their mess
It seems like everything is a mess these days &

no one wants to clean it up anymore
No one seems to take pride in a job well done &
I don't know if I can take it anymore
But my blood-type is Folgers Original &
we can drink as much coffee as we want for free
while on the clock so I guess it's not all that bad

The scarecrow ladies take their handbags &
defeated husbands when they leave
the wine glasses they leave behind
for us to clean up are drained
but they leave rocks glasses
full of suicide notes written in braille &
delusional promissory notes written on their receipts

Meanwhile, my phone keeps sending me push-notifications
from the only exes I genuinely miss
telling me what they really think of me &
I come to realize that I have changed for the better
in small increments over time
So I know that what they think of me is really
none of my business anyway &
we'd all be a lot happier if we didn't concern ourselves with
how were perceived by the people who shouldn't matter

Serving these mammals makes me feel like a wind-up doll
so I twist my man-bun tighter &
keep cleaning up other people's messes
But really I'm a sober bumblebee
but I don't serve a queen or have a colony
so I just keep collecting pollen & thin tips
to make honey to give away
in an attempt at lasting sanity

DENTIST

Don't make
small talk
with me
while your
fucking hands
are filling
my mouth

IT'S HARD

to
be
a
pacifist
in
the
land
of
the
gun

DRIVE-THRUS & SUPER-BOWLS

I see the warped minds of my
generation holding the reigns
fat off sucking marrow
from the brown bones of America
Over-educated & unemployable
distracted by manufactured
apathy & the mirage of plenty
Seeking wisdom in
organic-free-range-fair-trade-
coffee ground soothsayers
Shooting-up divinity
tryin' to catch the heavenly nod
while the Tower burns &
the wheel slowly turns
churning out cadavers
over there

Prestidigitation campaigns
brought to you by the
modern-day-makers-of-war

Anorexic-pre-teen-porno-queens
gagging on ambition
slinging self-loathing
while dirty kids ride
grain-cars west & south
with familiars & louse &
crystal-meth & wild-sweet-freedom
sharing rigs because
it doesn't really
fucking matter anymore

anyway now does it
they'll keep doling out fear
from the cathode ray
while some delve into
spiritual growth of yoga & tofu
Doing chi like drugs
never shutting up
always shutting down
Booting up computers &
cell phone & smack

Frightened of anything that don't look like him
can't even tell what he looks like anymore

With a gun in his mouth & tears in his eyes
unable to recognize it's his hand holding the gun
his finger on the trigger
His heart caged in gridiron & endorsements
circus-gladiator-man
Roman phalanx
concussion wealth
big house
big car
big dick
big deal

It's our mouths around the tailpipe
in open air
while burning coal
powers iPads

earthquakes & fire

There is lead in the water & in her hair

Medusa's daughters rove
looking for asylum
See them take shelter in
dreams of the homeless veterans
with baggy pants & no healthcare
who sleep under bridges down where
factory furnaces lie cold & dragons are too sick
to guard villages
The tinkerers are dead
the elementals are dead
the folk-heroes are dead
the cook-fire is dying

Please—
don't let the darkness in

WHAT VISION IS LEFT & IS ANYONE ASKING?

A cheap plastic container of about
500 thumbtacks came apart in my hands
The floor is awash with the lousy things

The classroom just down the hall ushers Amiri Baraka's
Somebody Blew Up America
with a cool subtle beat under it

Until my head swims in
The Tuskegee Syphilis Experiments

Crack-cocaine funding
CIA Contras in Nicaragua
under Reagan's watchdogs

You know,
Democracy in action

Weak knees on cheap carpeting
seems paltry against the oceans of history

I pick up the last of the tacks &
suck the meager blood from the tip of my finger
as I walk down the hall to peek into the classroom

The students look bored
          looking down into the scrying pool of their cell phones

Somebody did blow up America &
it seems like nobody cares

8 BY EIGHT

A pithy epitaph
A whistle in the darkness
A welcome companion for the trudge
A suture for the hungry wound
A luminous candle
A callous hand
A chaotic bed
A tended hearth

A cruel mask
A blistering revelation
A filigree dawn
A frenzied dirge
A ramshackle lament
A secret whisper
A public transgression
A leer into the void

A yellowed sneer
A menacing gratitude
A prayer of the hopeful
A foreboding countenance
A solitary ceremony
A crass promise
A hostile moxie
A concealment

A numb reprieve
A dime-store bauble
A venerable tinker
A sketchy gospel

A thrumming impulse
A corporeal abyss
A vapid filibuster
A pauper's tithe

A bit of magic
A small piece of light
A forbidden alchemy
A seedy long-shot
A medicine cabinet sepulture
A rotten vaccine
A faded platitude
A quivering voice

A cumbersome oath
A warped succor
A questionable panacea
A riddle vanguard
A threadbare illusion
A tooled scrimshaw
A tin idol
A struggling ziggurat

A venomous flower
A known pollutant
A salted garden
A truant lighthouse
A topical psalm
A broken pollinator
A hulking clemency
A foolscap brickbat
A nameless horror

A whittled god
A sylvan plague
A blooming fruit tree
A consecrated tribunal
A recycled lover
A gilded flower
A complicit scar
A secret intelligence
A necessity of living

Mother Whiskey said:
don't let your dreams get too cold
they won't keep that way

ON MAY 16TH 2005

My best & oldest friend
overdosed on fentanyl

At his funeral
I read a eulogy
high on that same drug

That's not even the
most shameful thing
I've ever done

In 1995

I got arrested for the first time
I got laid for the first time
it was a big summer for me

December 1999

I moved in with my
first serious girlfriend

For about a year
her grandmother thought
I was her cat
when her parents spoke my name

No one bothered
to correct her

In 2007

I got
blackout
piss-the-bed-fall-down
drunk

I came to
with broken ribs

I still don't know
exactly what happened

June 2013

A girl I had been dating
for close to a year
told me she was going home to
San Francisco for the summer

Two days after she left
I saw a picture of
her on Facebook
in Sofia
Bulgaria

She was kissing her
ex-boyfriend

I have never
felt
so
distant

In 2015

I had my first prostate exam
I discovered my first grey pube
it was a *very* big summer for me

In 1991

My mother didn't feed us soda

At my grandparents' fiftieth wedding anniversary
I drank soda after soda till I was sugar-headed
buzzing around with my cousins
we played sardines & held a séance
we climbed the great pine in the back yard

I climbed higher that day than
I have ever
before or since

I was coated in
sticky-sap
sand &
sweat

I remember bringing
something of heaven
down from the crown
of that tree

I can't seem to
remember
where I put it

I CALLED-IN SICK TWO DAYS IN A ROW THIS WEEK TO PLAY A GAME ON MY PHONE

Well, more accurately
I called in with car trouble
because I had already
called in sick this month
somehow, car trouble seemed
more believable

While we're on the subject
I called in with car trouble
because I didn't have it in me
to face the day

So, playing a game on my phone
was a sort of sanctuary
from depression

& I can't call in depressed
because, in my own twisted mind
I'm somehow too old for that

Depression isn't cute
with a greying beard

So, I favor the prudence of lies

RORSCHACH BLOTS

Sit in the tub till the water becomes cold
stare at the wall

Ponder the complexities of the
semicolon &
the weight of paper

Remember when you left
a four-color pen in your pants pocket
on wash day

How all your clothes were
spotted with ink—

        red
        green
        blue
        black

Remember that the dryer
was too   like Rorschach blots

it's apropos
a metaphor

Even when you try to
keep up on the mundane
tasks of living

Even when you try to
make things clean
you make a beautiful mess

ALL THE SCREENS BETWEEN US

I read an article in
Time about the
mental health issues
associated with
social media

specifically
how it's affecting
young people

There is a new
kind of human
suffering
garnered by
modernity

A wall of the mind
a border war
a blight of convenience

Brought upon us by
all the screens between us

MALADY LAKE
-for Lake Erie

The city cages the wind
& won't let it run free
Now it's feral   Coming off
the Lake hard & fast   Furiously
leaving rust, stained on the city
sidewalks like prison
graffiti

Lake Erie is sick
from the Steel Mill that
left poison to measure
absence   You can smell it
on its breath

Malady now
settled in the cold & dark
heart of the Lake

They warn against
swimming
the old waters

Yet it flows—
all the way to my
kitchen sink

RUSTY HIPSTERS

D.W.I. culture is fashionable
here in the Rust Belt

native hipsters
with interlock systems
in their Subaru's
only read Bukowski
      & call him Hank

like they are old drinking buddies
      & maybe they are

AT THE BUS STOP

He took us hostage
with his crazy bag-of-bananas
nettling like an allergen

Raving without humility
about lakes of fire
& the one true path

THE UNSPEAKABLE EVIL OF BILL STOLTE

Motherfucker
was
evil

We don't
talk about
it

The fool grapples cloud
a wise man accepts his place
cloud eludes the fool

UNFORMED CREATURE

In Wappinger Falls New York there is old magic
a Buddhist Monastery at the bottom of Overlook Mountain
with tattered prayer flags & a silent stillness
The temple is simple
monks tend the needs of this sacred place
In crimson & turmeric robes
with broken English through unbreakable smiles

Overlook Mountain is the southern most peak
of the Catskill Escarpment
it hides its own treasures
the hike is a couple hours up to the fire watchtower
less time back down   gravity's old trick
Purple sky reflects in mud puddles
from autumns final rain showers
Hidden around a bend in the path
so it seemingly materializes out of nothing
is the bones of an old hotel
only the concrete remains
Maples   some older than me
grow out of the dirt where a grand entrance
once welcomed the affluent
Once opulent fountains are full of filth & rain & garbage
moss covered stone & stair & wall   wet & complacent
fireplaces with remains some vandals or lost souls
seeking refuge in this abandoned place left behind
Spray paint scars the masonry
bright red & vulgar
much like my own scars
I feel akin to this place
Haunting   still   & broken

Up the mountain, there is a scenic overlook
where five or so states can be seen from
a cliff bluff, dropping off into the void
Conifers, as stately as anything human hands could build
stretch to the Hudson River
where Amtrak trains look like toys &
riverboats crawl along the thin vein
of life through this valley of commerce
Up here, where there are dates all the way back
to the 1800's carved into the rock shelf
none of these comforts can get to me
just the strength of the wind & vertigo
stirring something deep inside
something older than me
It is Beggar's Night, the night before
All Hallows' Eve, 2014
the saints watching quietly
we shamble down the mountain
in the moon's embrace
unafraid

Down the road from the Monastery
lies another holy place
Hallowed ground
The Chapel of the Sacred Mirrors
where a different kind of magic is born

It is Samhain
a woman
name of Ka
does a Serpent Feathers dance
that is something to behold
I am enthralled by the movements of this woman
part angel

part bird
all something you can't put words to
the music   ubiquitous
When Ka finishes her first dance
you can feel gooseflesh ebb across the room
Ka does another dance
slower
mesmerizing
She finishes her final dance
I look around
All the woman in the circle
surrounding the sacred space
are in tears
I feel nothing
there are men
also moved to tears from the beauty
or meaning in this dance
that I somehow couldn't gather

Like an unformed creature
I missed some enchantment
some brilliance
right in front of my rapt gaze
It's as if something hasn't matured in me
or has been neglected so long it's now
too rusty
too corroded
to move
too many moving parts
unmoved for
too many years

THE SUBTLETIES OF EVERYTHING

The morning has wooden bones as
I blend fresh root vegetables with
flash-frozen mixed berries that hide
seeds between my teeth for me to
discover throughout the day

I fold square paper into prayers &
sit quietly for a time then
go about the business of living

The afternoon has meerschaum bones
carved into scrimshaw dreams while
the music of combustion engines &
filthy slush fills the subtleties of everything
with a purpose-driven direction
I cannot seem to realize

I spit seeds into the corners
of the afternoon that
bloom into sharp things
until I'm surrounded

By the time the day runs out of heartbeats
all I've gathered is a little
more regret

THE SOLITARY WANDERINGS OF AN EXTROVERT

The first day of vacation left me feeling so restless
I decided to go see my friend with the harmonica

With only Sam Cooke, Diana Ross &
A Boy Named Sue for company I head east

Everyone in my rearview mirror is mad at me
for protecting my own interests—
just like them,

All the trees are sleeping to the lullaby of the
Susquehanna
NPR is a threadbare time machine

All the west-bound drivers are ghosts
wearing masks that look like you when you are
disappointed in me
a face I know too well

It's cold here but I like it
I keep better in the cold
I'm comforted by the constant
yellow service-engine-soon light on the dashboard
it's as if I have something in common with this old car

I get to Brooklyn & the driving
has my jaw clenched &
my knuckles white until
I'm greeted by a platoon of snowplows on 2nd Street
they are lining both sides of the road
like armored hoplites & I realize that it's all about

preparedness

That's the answer
have faith in the unknown & make ready

So I wander the slushy streets with impunity as
every Rude Boy in Brooklyn comes out
in their scally-caps & I notice
Brooklyn is caged-in fire escapes &
everything is an exquisitely beautiful & dirty matte grey

It's cold
my feet are wet &
I wouldn't change a thing

SISTER BARB

Would sit at the counter
roll silver
with the waitresses
working thirds

She was a kind
private woman

Barb listened

One day she didn't come in...

A group of volunteers—
went to clean up her home
cooks, bussers, servers
        no managers though

We found a life fractured by loss

Barb hadn't thrown anything away
since her husband died
piles of rubbish blocked the door

Take-out containers from the restaurant
        old ones, we hadn't had in years
        made a sort of strata in the kitchen
        layers & layers of food wrappers
        & packaging
        & maggots

She had piled adult diapers like an obelisk, or a ziggurat

used ones, taller than me
next to the broken toilet—

An alchemy of empathy &
disgust formed in my gut
while at the foot of this monument

A labyrinthine temple of filth
　　feline acolytes
　　& flies—

you've never
seen so many flies

All manner of things everywhere
creating thin paths through the house

I wanted to be strong
　　　　I wanted to help her

but the smell—
　　　there are no words
　　　no metaphor
　　　to do it justice
It smelled like grief

We filled dozens of contractor bags
without even finishing the kitchen

It was when I found her wedding dress
in the hall closet that I lost it
it was in a translucent
zipped-up dress bag
like a time-capsule

or a memory in a pensieve—
        untouched by the devils of loss

The next day it was decided
that we were out of our depth
so professionals were called

So they came & cleaned her house
& she came back
& rolled silver at the counter
with the third shift waitresses

I have never loved deeply enough to truly break
        I hope someday I can be strong like Barb
             & shatter

RUNAWAY

When I wore the
burning collar of youth
I learned how to hold
in the center of my palm
the smoldering ember of resentment

Papa taught me about
runaway truck ramps
on mountain roads
taught me how breaks fail

Careening trucks
use these ramps to stop

When I was gnawing the
burning collar
with no breaks—
out of control
careening down my own mountain

Papa taught me how to let go

JULY VALENTINE

I stopped offering up
silent prayers of gratitude &
began to sing a song of worry
until I was all out of metaphor so
I headed west in search of the
nameless madcap riddle &
a secret to divorce from self-pity

In the thrumming
green heart of America
the blameless eagle
was splayed in autopsy
in the unthinking lantern light
of a Kansas City Independence Day

Baptized with mirth &
sober backyard campfire smoke

In the—
wiz pop
            wiz pop
dazzle shower of
liquid fireworks
we began to outgrow fear

In Kansas City
they know how to celebrate
independence
they know what
independence means—
not preservation of mercurial freedom

from some imagined foreign oppressor
but freedom
from the bondage—
of self

-July 4th 2017

ANGER IS A DUBIOUS LUXURY OF NORMAL MEN

There is blood in the water again
it makes me sick with fear

Not fear of what will happen to me—
but fear of things I am capable of

THE HOLLOW HEART OF THE MOUNTAIN

The old mountain speaks in echoes
to argue with the ancient sky

about interpretations of the song the rain sings to
teach the young snow to dance

The flower only whispers metaphor
reaching for the sun with green fingers

of envy

blind to its own beauty

SLEEP PARALYSIS

I awoke & everything was honey

I awoke in honey, went to the bathroom, &

Awoke in honey, went to the bathroom, descended the stairs, &

Awoke in honey, bathroom, stairs, ran water for coffee, ground
beans, &

Awoke, honey, bathroom, downstairs, ground beans, went outside
to smoke in the dawn, &

Awoke, honey, pissed, descended, made coffee, went outside to
smoke in the burgeoning morning, got a cup of fresh coffee, &

Woke up, honey, pissed, descended, brewed, smoked, cup, went
back upstairs, &

Woke up, honey, piss, descend, coffee, smoke, cup, back upstairs,
began dressing for the day, &

Awoke, honey, piss, descend, coffee, smoke, cup, ascend, dressing
for the day, went to the bathroom again, &

I woke up & the darkness was on me, pinning me down, its
formless weight on my chest making breath a struggle, &—

I awoke tired & wary

That was months ago,
I spend every moment in fear that

I will
awaken

TO RESIST DESPAIR

Bug splatter from eleven states
obscured horizon where mountains
are birthed of wild-fire & cloudburst

We saw no vultures in sixteen
hours of barefoot desert
leading me to know—
it must be us

GREY BROTHER

I don't recall if I ever knew his name
but we broke bread together
where the guilty or the hopeful
make soup for the loathsome
& some of 'em even treated us with dignity

The soup line was called "Friends of Night People"
The name didn't sit right with me, it still don't

Night People, as if the daylight was not for us
Night People, nocturnal human scourge

The sun goes down &
Ollie Ollie Oxen Free

The broken slink out from their hovels

The downtrodden crawl out
from under the city's bootheel
to clean up your discarded aluminum cans

Friend, from the Indo-European root meaning "to love"

I know there is love

Perhaps that's what compels the sweating ladle-maidens
to pour out their boiled compassion into
single servings of salted hope

Perhaps compels the youth groups
to make their monthly pilgrimages

to see god's own children first hand
so they can open their young hearts
invite understanding to move in &
unpack for the long stay

Look for god in the wet eyes
of the veteran begging for change
pocket or otherwise

Look for god in the eyes
that read the runes of the ground
cracked sidewalk
flowering weeds
glittering broken things
You have to work for it
to catch even a glimpse of those darting eyes
but it's worth it, trust me

My grey brother was one of those—
brim of his oily ballcap guarding his bowl
dipping stale bread in silence

Never a word

He would walk away with his head down
reading the dead language of earth

Today as I drove
to my own troublesome blessings
I saw my old grey brother
walking tall in his bright yellow
working-man's vest
gathering fallen branches &
other people's carelessness

to collect them in the sturdy bed
of an Olmstead Parks Department Services
crusty John Deer Utility Vehicle
in Delaware Park near Hoyt Lake

It is the doing that we find purpose

Keep your head up grey brother
walk tall in the morning sunlight
& recognize me only
as friend

FEET OF CLAY

Looking to the ground
ashamed of sun
averted eyes see only ends
Yet perfect little god-bodies
wither in the river
stepped in never twice

Yet things all require
purpose
shiver
structure
movement

Or points of articulation
frozen
taken by attrition
or avarice
broken on the crest of desire

What would dream be on a distant satellite?
Would it be the same if you
were not folly
& they not farce?

Thinking yourself different is
perhaps what makes you the same
Like clone
like mirror

Being wrong is a universal human condition

IT AIN'T ALTRUISM IF IT'S FOR AN AUDIENCE

Everything I know about service
I learned from a convincing liar

THE ROAD FROM HELL IS PAVED WITH SERVICE

Find comfort in usefulness because—
the past is a horror that keeps on giving

FIRST, SHOOT THE ALLIGATORS CLOSEST TO THE BOAT

Do what is in front of you
you will be contacted

FAULT FINDER

This old bastard has a blackhead in his ear
that appears to have been forming
since before I was born into the earth
I can't stop looking at it
it's magnificent, hypnotic & gross

Then I realize—
I haven't heard a word he's said
I was too focused
on his imperfections

MERCHANT

They say there is wisdom in acceptance
that there is peace to be found in surrender
as if things have & always will
be just as they are

Some things will never be acceptable
cost what they may
Some commonalities in
this culture shouldn't be norms

Some things will follow
tenacious like student loans
Relentless— Revenant
like shadow

The function of the poet is to interpret
the language of the heart
to split the wishbone
between the hopeful & the damned

To never keep
the larger portion
To dole out wishes
real or imagined

The poet keeps one eye
in another world
to see the omens
Real or imagined

makes no difference
Real or imagined

This Cycloptic vision to lessen
the burden of the heart
by piecemealing themselves away
Some poets deal in lead

If you meet the ones who
cast no shadow
the ones who never blink
Don't hold their gaze

for they are hungry ghosts
merchants of emotion
not all of which are
pure or gentile

The poem is an attempt
to lessen the burden on the heart
by offering small parts of self
up on the alter

The heart is where the soul
rests in the living

When the heart is weighed
against the Feather of Truth
at life's end—
between this place & the next

when drawn from the deep well of slumber
into the whatever that follows
if the heart is too heavy
it will be eaten by the crocodile

Be sure your heart is not burdened
& heavy with acceptance

PERNICIOUS GOD

who will deliver us if
god made us in his image?

god of filth
god of compost
god of excess
god of landfills
god of junk

god of the hoard
god of the bog
god of plenty
god of fuck
god of drunkards

god of fugue
god of pathos
god of fisting
god of megrim
god of over-medicated

god of the brave
god of the oil spill
god of fracking
god of toxic algae blooms
god of pesticides

god of petroleum
god of fecundity
god of aggression
god of the three-fifths compromise
god of chemistry

god of disproportion
god of the drive-thru
god of engineered famine
god of the bomb
god of superiority

god of the scarab
god of rendered lard

god of free-radicals
god of us vs. them

no—
we've made god

in the image of what
we're not

When we fuck it's like
a Jackson Pollock painting
without the value

STAY HUNGRY, STAY FOOLISH

Keep your powder dry
You'll need it

Lace up—
trudge softly
where fireflies
light the path

Carry
in a
cupped hand
your origami
paper-heart

In the night
in the moments
you don't know if
you are awake or not

gather your
leftover treasures

garner them
to the
filigree shallows
of slumber

Keep your paper-heart dry
as you drown your riches
in brackish waters

ROSE OF JERICHO

I believed I could
light the candle

before
the match burned
down

Singeing my fingers

Now I think
that maybe
some things
are better left

given up

ONCE AGAIN BE CLEAR

When my ears popped
at twelve-thousand feet
above sea level

I imagined that's what
kissing you would be like

The subtly built up discomforts
would suddenly disappear
senses would attune
to new heights &
the music of the world would
once again be clear

MAKE TIME FOR TEA

It's a ten traffic jam kind of week & I'm bone tired
but there's honest work yet to be done

Like the quiet scent of your shampoo that lingers
as you move to the kitchen to attend the kettle's whistle

Like your tongue, thick with ginger

But the day comes apart in my hands
& woman—
I just want to do right by you

IN THE WAY BACK OF MY MOTHER'S BORROWED CARAVAN ON A MIDNIGHT MIDSUMMER DRIVE THROUGH ILLINOIS

It's dark here
I'm with my love

The moon is a
cataract glass eye
looking through
with indifference

Some forgotten gods
are sending Morse Code
love poems
written in heat lightning
across the night

Trying in vain
to recapture the
adoration of children
grown & embarrassed

My love stirs
in her peaceful dream—
catching
with the butterfly net of slumber
the simple mercies
we outgrow everyday

Hold them darling—
while I keep watch
against the night
awaiting the dawn

I KEPT THE ENGINE RUNNING FOR HER

She put me
on the backburner

BOOTS & TIGHTS

When she walked by
a big bang in my chest

formed galaxies

Every constellation—
her face

MCLOVIN' IT

When
I think
about
Love
I think
about
McNuggets

Sure,
it's a thing
& people do it
but
do you
really think
that's
a good idea?

YOU FUCKED UP

I would
        have
walked
        through
the Fire
        with
you

HE BET THE RENT ON LOVE

He chose poorly

I WAS TRYING TO CONVINCE MYSELF THAT I COULD BE GOOD FOR YOU

A celestial thumbprint
at the moment of birth
a still frame of the clockwork universe
immutable laws of an infinite God

Omnipotence has short memory
& long life

Unleavened spirit
like a starship in a bottle
confined by imagined limitations

self-imposed
&
handed down
like
bad genes
&
student loans

An inheritance
I've refuted
not my birthright
as if
anyone
is responsible for
impressing
their worth on
anyone
but themselves

EAST RIVER IS NOT A RIVER, IT'S AN ESTUARY, BUT
EAST ESTUARY JUST DOESN'T HAVE THE SAME
RING TO IT & OTHER LIES THAT SOUND
BETTER THAN THE TRUTH

It's not you, it's me
I can quit anytime I want
I'm fine, don't worry
Sure, I've been tested
I'm not gunna lie
Yes, I'm certain
Believe me—

I love you

Nathanael William Stolte is the author of six chapbooks most recently, A Beggars Prayer Book (Night Ballet Press, 2017) & Ramshackle American (Analogue Submissions Press, 2018). Nathanael is a gamer, an educator, and a believer in the absurd. He was voted best poet in Buffalo (Artvoice, 2016). He is a madcap, flower-punk, D.I.Y. Buffalo bred & corn-fed poet. He responds to emails at nathanaelstolte@yahoo.com

Thank You!

Nathanael would like to thank the publications where some of these poems have previously appeared. *Five 2 One Magazine #thesideshow; The Rising Phoenix Review; Rusty Truck Zine; Ghost City Review Vol. 4 & Vol 5; Your One Phone Call; Mutata Re-Vol III & IV; Trailer Park Quarterly; Foundlings Vol 3; Poets Speak: While They Still Can; Punch Drunk Press; Thimble Magazine; Blue Mountain Review; Gasconade Review; Elm Leaves Journal.* Nathanael would also like to thank Osage Arts Community for affording him the space to create. This book would not be possible without the help of the following people: Jeanette Powers for her staunch dedication to the arts; John Dorsey for keeping the fire lit; Mother Richter for loving him when he was most unlovely; Dr. Peter Ramos for teaching him how to English. And of course Maj Ragain who taught Nathanael to kiss the joy as it flies so he may live in eternity's sunrise and to make honey out of old failures.

9 781950 380138